Sunbeam Machine

poems by
Cora Grey Huot

ISBN Paperback: 979-8-218-17994-6

Yellow Robin Books printing April 01, 2023

Yellow Robin Books and colophon are registered trademarks.

10   9   8   7   6   5   4   3   2   1

Edited by Rachele Huot

Front cover illustration by Cora Grey Huot
via Midjourney, Inc.

Printed in the U.S.A.

For my pet dinosaur,
who never left my side,
who wrecked the round table
and gobbled up its pride.

For my closest friends,
who think I am quite strange,
who see me talking to ants,
and dancing in the rain.

And finally,
for my sisters, my brothers,
my friends, and my foes;
for the many people I love dearly,
and the billions I have yet to know :

Don't grow up.
Be all that you want.
Be as open as the sky
and as bright as the sun.
Don't think you're too mighty,
too proud, too old, or too honed,
to let go of it all and just have fun.

Contents

Sunbeam
Machine

Robin

My grandma calls me robin
but not because I sing.
She says I am most myself
whenever I am free to swing -
to fly high and touch the sky
or to dip low beneath the trees -
like a honey-headed bumble bee.

　　She would watch me go,
　　chuckling behind her rosy cheeks,
　　whenever I hit that childhood flow -
　　playing pretend with my colorful friends -
　　chasing dreams and giving cheerful shrieks.

She calls me robin,
but not because I am free.
She says I am always sailing
upon puddles that are seas -
the choppy slush that I love so much
where I make my boats from leaves -
like a silly salmon swinging in lemon tea.

　　She used to poke my belly
　　and I would light up like a star,
　　where there I would roll around,
　　stopping once or twice for more,
　　like a thief stealing from a honey jar.

Dragons of the Holly

Lizards in a bush, they say,
     really have all the fun.
They bob their heads
     and run real fast along
     the holly run.
They gloat to their foes
     and wink at new ladies,
     even though a lady knows
     a sly lizard is a skink.

Their scant scaly hides
     give me something to believe in,
     for even in my mind
     I know they could be dragons.
I imagine, how might they bob
     their noses at the sky?
Might their wings
     be silly or grandeur or thorny?

How wondrous they might
     all seem to be, when they could
     soar above the shadows of the sky,
     getting fat with delight
     and dark as night,
     to sunbathe all day.
Might they chase the sun,
     thinking the earth no feat
     of wing? I imagine that

is what they dream.
Outside my transparent window,
  the holly bush reveals
  all to my little eyes.
To the lizards and skinks,
  the holly is like their castle,
  a pokey thorny keep.
They can climb all day
  and dip their heads in play,
  as if the weather
  was never better.

Sunbeam Machine

I am a sunbeam machine,
grinnin', an' eye-twinklin', an' being
a silly alien thing.
When my clothes are all torn,
an' my toes are dark green,
make no mistake,
I am as clean as can be.

I am a golden human bean,
a breakfast eatin', an' belly burpin',
stomach submarine.
When my body feels full,
an' when my face has a jelly sheen,
I will take to the backyard
and drum on my sun-kissed tambourine.

I am a raucous, ramblin', paradin' scene,
singin', an' dancin', an' twirlin',
a artistical musical dream.
When my head gets all dizzy,
an' my legs cross in-between,
into the holly I will tumble
and fuss up my new jeans.

I am a mess, but I feel I am queen,
crawlin', an' diggin', an' collectin'
tiny pieces of dopamine.
When my pockets are full of treasure,

an' my palms are clamped delicately,
I will bring this lizard into the den
and make my mother scream.

          I am in trouble, in a room of hot steam,
            yellin', an' complainin', an' shakin',
              my mother thinks I am obscene.
           When my feet tracked in grass
         an' my jeans have three torn seams,
            I get the scoldin' of a lifetime,
             and the lizard I must fling.

                    I am grounded, "outdoor-weaned,"
                 sulkin', then snickerin', an' glowin.'
                    No such thing as quarantine.
                 When I return to my window,
                 I will unlatch the broken screen,
                slip out through the holly bush,
              escaping my punish-mean.

          I am a free bird an' a wild thing,
        grinnin', an' laughin', an' playin'
             forever with routine.
           When I get it in my head
          that nothing can intervene,
       I am like a piglet in a lake of mud,
      an oinkin', rootin' tootin,' squealin'
           sunbeam machine.

Haley-go-round

Haley and her sweat-stained shirt
grips an iron bar.
She runs and runs and runs all day
never getting far.

Her feet are slick with mud and grass,
her pants are covered in grime.
She must persist, she must go on,
for this is the only time -
the time is now, to cast them out
to send the prisoners all about -
she must go on! She must win!
She will go on until her legs give out.

She runs quickly with toes flinging up,
with hands that are slick, deftly clinging tough.
"Go, Go, Go!" they cry, their voices high and pitched
until Haley herself hops onto the wild mix.

Thus she rides, at one with speed,
adherently gripping colorful iron bars.
Soon it was, that the remaining three,
flung off like rockets to Mars.

But Haley persists victorious, joyfully.
She glues herself with arms, legs and chest,
spinning round and round, again and again,
until finally she loses all her zest.

Palm Pilot

Foul weather.
It reminds me
of the child I still am,
running, laughing
grasping at wind.

I like to play coy
like a root stuck, earthed.
Disregarding my limbs,
I wishfully believe
my legs are stronger
than their girth.

A tropical storm
is really quite the frenzy,
but I make more fun
playing palm tree pilot
in my rain-soaked onesie.

Hurricane Vacation

A vacation?
   In the middle of the school year?
Sign me up, I don't care,
   take me wherever my dear.

A four hour drive
   to the Georgia state line.
Are we going to six-flags?
   Is that why we packed our bags?

A fancy hotel,
   do they have a pool?
Ew! What is that smell?
   My dad says its mildew,
     time for a new room.

It's pouring outside.
   Raining cats and mice.
or is it dogs and lice?
   Mother says either way,
     no going outside.

Can we turn on the tube?
   Can I watch some cartoons?
My sisters say there is a hurricane
    on the loose. Avoid the news.

Will the house sink into muck?

What of my things, my toys?
On a good note,
    I will say goodbye to my good clothes,
        "awe shucks, what bad luck."

For only one night,
    there is a bundle of mixed sighs.
Though my dad won us
    three plushies from a machine,
the trees outside violently sneeze.

Orangutan

Today I went to the zoo,
    to see a mocking bird.
        My friends, they laughed,
            and pulled me along
                to see the most absurd.

Creatures with fuzzy bodies
    who laze all day in the sun,
        "Oh I wish I was a lion," one said.
            "They have it easy being lazy,
                no one dares to wake them up."

I nod my head, "I guess that's true,
    but they also eat zookeepers like me and you."
        I got a pat, for being too blunt,
            and so we continued on at the zoo.

Slithering snakes as green as a pear,
    coiled up like a hose beneath a lamp.
        It blinked real slow, bored with its show,
            though it gave some a fright,
                and soon we followed the flow.

An enclosure for an orangutan.
    How alike and orange and limber!
        How does he enjoy watching us,
            hanging upside down, or right side up?
                How fantastic and careless and free!
                    Well, as free as he can be.

The others laugh as he stands on his head.
I thought at once that he has it right
by watching the world in a gleeful fashion.
I tried at once to retain his passion,
but as soon as I tried
to stand on my head,
I was mocked and ridiculed,
when my pants split a thread.

Shy Light

Sparks
that drive
social games,
I haven't a clue
how they work.
I'm adequate
at best to say
the fires in my
heart today
peer behind
those
doors.

It's a brave thing to peek
behind my
own facilities,
to find out what
all the fuss is,
to open wide
and connect eyes
with strangers
on the street.

They come and go,
to where I do not know,
making repetitive remarks -
about the weather, their moods,
or their imaginary arcs -
and talking, always
yapping, like
a poodle
with no remorse.

Playing Attention

Hark hark!
>> That's my part!
> I must not forget it.

>> Hark hark!
>>> That's my part!
>> I really wish I had more to say.

>>> Hark Hark!
>>>> It rhymes with shark shark!
>>> How silly it would be to swim and hark.

Hark Shark!
> Or is it Hark Hark?
Does a shark hark or does it bark?
>> Maybe a hark is like a lark?
>>> A lark in a park…

>> Park Lark!
>>> I'm sure it's true.
> Or maybe it's more like blue swede shoes.
>>> What is swede and why are they blue?
>>>> Does a lark bark with blue shoes too?

>>> Lark Bark!
>>>> That's my part?
>> I know it's coming up soon.

> OH! There it is!
>> My part at last.
> I shall give it my all.
>> My mum will be so proud!

BARK BARK!
> That's my part.
I didn't forget it.
> I really am so smart.

Sass in Class

My class is full of sass.
I really wish time would pass.
While Johnny picks on Suzy,
her friends call him "crass."

The teacher blames Suzy,
who only meant to laugh,
while Thomas sneaks away
licking his roll of grass.

I really wish
this class would pass
into obscure oblivion,
like entropic gas.

Gary likes to kick my desk,
and Victor dreams of Mass.
Improbable is our attention
on Miss Carter, alas.

My class is full of frass,
I would blame Thomas, but cannot,
for he stepped outside the glass -
out into the yard,
covered in dew drop strass.

Merrily Merrily

Fairly merrily,
a multitude of
eerily bilberry fairilies
dance on primarily strawberrilies.

Wearily, and arbitrarily,
they fairily, hairily, and customarily
jump and shout voluntarily.

They sing with glee
and always unwarily,
contrarily disregarding
giant hands scooping
militarily, merrily.

Easy-bake Robot

Once I ate a can of beans;
they gave my tummy
quite a start.

But when I flipped
the red button switch
to make some chilli stew,
I produced a black bean
gooey-thing: a tart.

How odd and off the cart.
Why did I produce
this bean filled tart?

Oh I see,
because the lever
on the receiver
was flipped to art.

Pancakes

Insects stir from their slumber.
The birds chirp, singing broadway songs,
as clock hands twirl on prongs.
Still under blankets, encumbered.

Bees harvest nectar from pink cowpea.
Inside my mind, a sprightly stroll
past raging rivers and fire troll.
A subconscious topography.

A pip of fear, yet I refuse to awaken,
despite the morning cooking oil,
breakfast cooking on an iron coil.
Still under wraps, I won't be shaken.

Vivid, verdant jungles, tower in the middle.
Spotted leopards growl with lust.
My feeble mind must smell robust
climbing the tower's stairwell twiddle.

A doorway opens up, blazing light.
A sun spark begins burning. Squinting,
feet continue moving, sprinting.
Bedroom warming with morning light.

Rousing free from cotton cocoon,
scent of pancakes in the galley.
Stretch the body, mini pep rally,
my stomach growls a jaguar tune.

I Don't Like You

I really did not voice
my opinions on royalty.
I should have told her
to find another,
but the role was
already filled: me.

A red-haired girl said to me
"I am your new queen, king."
I guess I had no choice
when she started pushing
me on the swing.

She said to me,
"I adore thee, all forever
with my wholest
of wholly hearts."
I didn't like that she kept
pushing me higher.
Nor that my belly began to depart.

She came around my house
and kicked me in the thigh.
She said I ought to treat her well
and that kings don't really cry.
She really thought I played along
about the communion we never shared.
I wish I never sent her a letter:

my first poem about a bear.

She asked me one day
"Are you gay?"
I said "I don't really know.
I don't see people like I do bees,
or trees or leaves and such.
You really ought to give up this crown
that's got your knickers in a bunch."

She cocked her head and looked real cross,
kicked my shin and stormed off.
Some how I did feel a little bit blue.
Perhaps it was those ten days together
when she didn't catch my cues.

Soda Stub

Bounding to the kitchen again.
It is filled to the brim with
sweets and crunchy treats.
The only issue is, of course
my mother stacked them
on the tallest rack.

How am I to get up there?
I can barely lift a chair.
Maybe I can climb
like a monkey on a vine,
but not with mother
standing behind my back.

Sugar, sweets,
that is what my monster's
hunger craves to eat.
There must be something.
Anything. May the heavens
send me a gooey,
no-good-for-me crop.

Miracles do happen!
My father left the kitchen
and in his wake, a fizzy shake,
one that I will take like a snake.
His half empty soda pop!

Oh yes, oh glee!
My mother says if the can
is not empty, the rest is for me!

I must impress
the joy in my chest
when my lips were
pressed on the rim.
But when I drank
from that treasured pop,
I really got my wish.

My tongue shriveled up
and my monster dropped.
I even heard the swish.
A cigarette butt in the drink
turned the fun fizz to black skim.

Fire Flume

In the summer
when everyone is queer,
teetering on springy animals,
there is one thing that all must know:
the metal chute is off limits.
Don't think twice about saying no.

And yet…
My friends and I took turns to dare,
turning our joys from the swings.
Each of us regarded the sign
above that vile metal thing.

"I bet you wouldn't.
I dare you to touch.
Go down on the slide,
just this once."

What happened at first,
on that hot aluminum sheet,
came the steam from bare skin
and the singe on blue jeans.

I thought myself brave,
but more than pressured to try.
I thought of how the victory,
and the slide, would be mine.
But when I sat down,
placing trust in my pride,
the slide turned to magma
and I learned how to fly.

Attack of the T-Rex

Quick! Hurry!
Close up the keep!
A monster is coming!
A monster as big as ten me's!

Go! Faster!
Set forth your silver mauls!
Draw up the bridge!
Send marbles through the halls.

Steady, ignite,
get ready, FIGHT!
There it is! A dragon!
Or is it a lizard?
Sire, I think it's called
a dinosaur?

No matter. Batter!
Keep its hungry tongue off the walls.
It gobbled up double sword Sam
and trampled the village dolls.

Oh blast! I forgot!
This castle has no rear!
We'll be eaten in mere moments
unless we gather all spears!

Points forward, all together!
Don't hesitate to get rough.
After all we're all just plastic
and that beast is made of fluff.

Fire Ants

Sugar ants are black and small
they like to march and gather.
Whenever I have an accident
they always eat the splatter.
Fire ants, however…

Those blazing red insects
with fire engine hides -
their orange-red little bellies
filled with molten venom -
never care if you're big or small
they really love to bite.

They love to gather seeds
and climb the sweetgum trees,
to hunt and claim shiny lizard scales
as treasure for their queen.

They are so adept at crafting
they make their burrows
without congestion or draft.
If it floods and their mounds turn to mud
they simply build a fire ant raft!

It really is a shame though
to live beside such foe.
When I mow the lawn for chores
they crawl out with bodies burning bright.
Into battle they thrust their corps
and send me screaming back indoors.

Iguana Picnic

Days at the beach were never rare;
my family loves the sun,
the tropical turquoise ocean,
the hunt for sea glass and shells,
pocketing more than one.
What took the cake
though, were the locals
and I'm not talking about people.

Iguanas as far as we could tell,
took up lodging anywhere they could.
They usually had a cold, a cough,
a wheeze, a sneeze. I thought
they must be miserable things.
Always sick, never clean.
Do they hold their mucus in
to make their skin turn green?

With a whoop, a hiss,
they saunter through sand
and make their striped tails swish.
Hundreds of iguanas, all taking
the good spots on the shore.
They click and yip,
with fleas they scritch,
and if I was not careful,
if I turned my back just once,
they often ran off with
my peanut jelly sandwich.

The Greatest Show

The greatest show
that I have ever seen
were a thousand streaks of blue and white,
on a heavy humid night,
filled to the brim with broken light.
I talk, of course, of lightning.

Upon the roof of my
best friends home,
ill-advised by his mother,
I watched for an hour
the wild thrash of power,
the tearing of molecules
molding cumulus like soft loam.

With a dash of blue
and purple energy, too,
my skin turned all attention
to the drums in the sky,
which boomed in my lungs,
as the hairs on my head
flew off with goodbyes.

The greatest show
I have ever known
did not include the circus,
or their multicolored flare.
For the best show on earth,
I estimate its worth,
left me scratching my head
and the smell of burnt hair.

Loitering

Round and round,
another lap around
the newest shopping mall.

My friends and I
love to pass by
for our goal is never to stall.

Round and round,
another lap around
to the food court for a nibble.

Samples to eat,
which are always free,
for we haven't any pebbles.

Round and round,
another lap around,
we must have walked three miles.

So we stopped our feet,
found a nice seat,
while a cop came up in a rile.

He said he's seen us
going round and round,
and said we were exploiters.

If not for my friend's mum
who startled his qualm,
we would have been two loiterers.

Fruit from a Rosebush

A bramble of barb-like horns
picked my finger so.
I know they meant no harm,
but I couldn't help but kick
and yelp and say mean things
to that thicket of thorns.

My pa says it is a rosebush
but in all the years
since I have lived here,
not once have they bloomed
or given colorful jewels,
except the fabric from my tush.

Then there came a violent storm.
It battered the garden
with winds that whipped,
rain that broke upon
the thicket with vengeful scorn.

By the next sun,
I saw that it was beat.
I asked my pa, could it be saved?
He felt, in earnest, that it might be,
but we also wondered about the tree -
the verdant stump that gave us blooms,
but nothing more than fickle things.

I watched from afar,
for I was still a wee bean,
as my pa took up the spade
and went to work for three days
in a battle between bramble,
brawn and brain.

By the third day he was torn,
his gloves trashed, his boots
shredded, like his arms.
I said nothing, but I knew he had won,
confirmed by the next spring,
where blossomed two from divided horn.

First grew the green noses,
which then soon turned yellow,
and when the humid summer hit,
we harvested oranges by the basketfuls.
The best part of it all, though,
between sweet bites of zest,
in the corner of the garden
bloomed seven white roses.

Pulling Weeds

One, two, three, four,
pulling weeds by the root.
Make them pop, make them drop,
stop, droop, and stoop.

Five, six, seven, nine,
Oops, I passed one!
Sorry to miss you little guy.
I was so busy counting,
I left a patch a mile wide.

Eight, ten, eleven, again,
in the spring, weeds have no end.
I'm really tired, I must stop.
Oh, they've grown,
there goes my weekend.

Absolutely Not

Are they done yet now?

No, says my mum.

When will the blueberry muffins
be ready to eat?

In an hour, quit pestering me.

But mum, they are there
on the countertop,
steaming, gleaming,
with crumbles on top.
They look pretty ready to me.

You've not eaten your breakfast,
and most of these are for mass.
Go wash your face
and get ready for Sunday class.

But mum, I've done all that.
I washed my hands
and put shoes on my feet.
I even had time to brush my teeth.
Can't I have a muffin now?

If you brushed your teeth,
don't you think,
it's already too late
to have a snack or treat?

First Kiss

It doesn't make sense,
this thing called "first kiss."
All my friends explain
it's a necessary thing.

Here I sit,
the fifth in a dugout,
nodding my head while
my friends goad me on.
I don't understand why
they are so invested,
or why they think me wrong.

My first fling,
a "girl friend,"
walks in circles around
a baseball diamond.
With her best friend in tow,
they talk and stare
from first base.
I can tell I'm missing something.

"A kiss is when your
lips touch. Like this."
They bump two fists.
"But why must that be?
How is that affection,
that, I cannot see."

"Friend," they tell me,
"It's been two weeks."
"Three actually."
"All the more reason to kiss
during this special season."
Do they mean Hallow's Eve?

What's it matter anyhow?
I only know her skills in math.
Why do they persist?
They got me wrinkled up dry
when they insist on this silly kiss.

I don't feel at all about this.
The dugout sure is
feeling like timeout.
I've got to get out
while they shake
their defeated heads.

I'm all worked up,
I will admit.
I would rather walk back
home and dismiss
this absurdity called,
"first kiss."

Jump

One day
        there was a fight
and I was right in the middle.
        I'm afraid to say,
I got in trouble
        for something my friend did today.

These kids pushed the blame
        and narrowed me into a mix.
Even though I did no wrong,
        they sought to take me
one to twenty-six.

I thought I was a goner,
        but by luck I had a lizard brain.
I ducked and weaved
        between punches and kicks,
to defend my feeble armor.

They called me names
        and tried to throw shame,
even as they went for my face.
        But I will admit
I was pretty quick
        and jumped right out
of the frame.

Sharp Student

There is this game in class,
      which really felt like a club.
A competition to see who's best
      at whittling their pencil down to nub.

A kid named Drew started it up
      and soon the back row joined in.
We thought grammar wasn't much
      so we went to sharpen our wins.

Mike was the first to break his in half
      he got too close to the lead.
Terrell came pretty close to winning
      but Drew's was down to eraser head.

I thought I could succeed,
      though the others said I was daft.
I strode up to the auto-sharpener
      to grind yellow wood toward shiny brass.

Drew was astonished,
      one more twist and he was beat.
But when I went to go again,
      I broke the sharpener and got a new seat.

Just Me

What do you want to be
when you grow up?
An age old question,
doesn't it suck?

Here comes Sam,
asking me again and again.
"What will you be,
except an older twerp?"

I would rather not be
anything, really.

"What do you want to do?
What about your career?"
My friends all have picked -
a firefighter, a rock star,
even a civil engineer.
But these are all just jobs
that cannot define me.
It is quite confusing,
more so when they laugh at me.

"What do you want to do,
will you be a sailor, a teacher?
Will you feed leopards at the zoo?"
All those sound nice,
but it is not really 'me.'

Though I would rather
do anything except go to sea.

"What do you want to be? Tell me!
A princess, a doctor,
a travelling one-man band?
Will you choose to be a parent
or be a beach bum with a tan?"

I do not think it's time
to choose any number of these.
Here, where I am,
I'm happy just being free.

"That is rather dull.
You are really quite short-sighted.
With no career or identity
you will never be delighted."

I know that's not true.
Sam is just playing her tune.
I find the most comfort, see,
when I give my attention
to the lizards in the trees.

"But what will you actually grow up to be?!"

Just…me.

Conspiracy Clock

I think the clock has stopped,
it might as well be arrested.
Whenever there's a history exam
it always quickens up.
I think it should be tested.

There it goes again,
ten minutes too slow.
I swear the teacher turns it off
the hands are all congested.

I turned it round,
when no one watched,
and watched insects crawl out.
It was quite infested.

I tried my friends watch,
and the clock at lunch,
I swear it's not just a hunch.
The whole school is invested.

Outside, Inside

The bell rings
the toll of the iron ding.
Time to shout,
"School's out!
School's out!"

Two months to swing
and get fat on crispy treats.
Two months to play
and run wild all about.

Time to jump,
to play hoops and lump
on the couch with the telly.
Maybe I will even grow some leaves
like a mossy, swampy stump.

I must begin at once to list
all the ncw adventures
that I have missed.
To call my friends
and ask them questions
and get all of their summer reflections.

Oh, what's that?
It's August again?
Ah shucks. Ah guts.
School is back in session.

Beachfront Property

War on all sides!
The queen demands a moat!
Dig deep past the crust
use the wood from the bridge,
just make this castle float.

"My lady, my quest,
said the lord to her crest.
"Our castle is but sand.
We have got to descend
and send our builders more inland."

"Don't give me no fuss,"
said the queen who did thus.
"Send troops to the rafters
and pails with huge mops.
As long as the water splashes,
the digging must not stop!"

"But my empress, my queen,
we have but dug twenty-a-trough.
At this rate we are doomed,
the water is salty and looms,
the keep is sure to drop."

"But there is the ocean,
not some single whirlpool wave.
We can last forever

so long as the moat does not cave."

"Dear ruler, fair and just,
have you forgotten
why we are truly kaput?"

"Please tell me this
my lord, and quiet that tapping foot!"

"Sorry my friend,
I must amend.
To answer, then:
the giantess who built us
has gone away for good.
We have no builder for the moat
nor the means to make a boat."

"Aye," mused the queen,
"I see now that it is so.
Take shelter lord friend,
this is the end.
By children's hands we were built
and by undertow we shall go."

Alligator in the Sink

All at once, a two sister pile up
while I was wandering past,
on my way to fill my cup
from the kitchen drink.

They hooted and hollered.
While one scooped up a broom
the other donned a pair of gloves
and closed her collar.

I filled my cup
to the brim with pop,
checking once for no slop,
and began to pass once more.

My sisters screamed,
"Get it! Please!"
"There's an alligator
crawling on its belly,
slinking in the sink!"

I thought it strange
for a wild beast to behave,
crumpling up a thirty-foot tail
to hunt prey where one shaves.

When I did step inside
to see the beast in the sink,
I laughed until I cried,
for it was just a skink.

Leap Frog

Outside a humid culvert,
soaking in the summer mist,
clings a lime green frog
who sticks to the sides
with voluminous grips.

I named it.
Of course I did.
Leaping Liz was my new muse.
My amphibian friend that slowly blinked,
"Is this giant, friend or prey?"
but in my mind its eyes said "hey."

I was so giddy and full of green
I burst inside with rain touched feet,
slipping and sliding, loudly
announcing to my family,
"There's a frog outside the porch screen!"

My dad then plucked Liz from the pipe
and held her out for me to touch.
Bursting with anxious mirth,
I held my hand out hesitantly as such.

But instead, Liz leaped at my head
and I couldn't help but freak.
I clutched at my face,
while my sister laughed,
and I gave a strident shriek.

Carnival Gold

Come one, come all!
Come see the show!
The ecstatic, erratic,
eclectic, electric,
the carnival-tastic
show of the century!

Forget your worries,
forget your follies.
Leave behind your mind
but remember your kiddies, please.

Tickets, here!
Twenty bucks a pair.
Go on and see,
the fantastically frantic!
The funny-dumbs
and the kettle drums!

Step right up,
test that puny arm!
See those bottles, hun?
Knock em dead,
shock me alive,
and win a crown for your head!
Ohh! Too bad, kid.
The ball must be lead.

Don't be shy,
I see your eyes!
I bet you're a champion,

a keen-eyed sword!
Drop this ball into a circle
and claim the dragon's hoard!
Oh! Too bad there kid.
Shoo! On to the next bid.

Come fast, through fog.
Dodge the zombies
and cerberus,
the three-headed dog!
Slay the serpent
who constricts the exit.
Hurry on sport,
there are others waiting.
Go on! Leg it!

The final game,
the one for the glory.
Shoot that alien
and save humanity!
Go! Go! Don't be slow!
Water guns sure are fun!
Oh! What do ya know!
You won a carnival gold…
fish, that is.

Best run on home,
to find your mum.
I'm sure she will just adore
your glorious score.

"Oh…another chore."

The Last Roll

There comes a time
when dinner plates are cleaned,
the pitcher of lemonade is dripped dry,
and the old folk are nearly done
expending their stories of genes.

> A time of huffs and puffs
> after grandpa falls asleep.
> Those who are left to poll,
> with unsatiated tongues,
> begin to ponder the final question:
> "Who gets the last roll?"

> > It is an odd game we like to play.
> > Whomever asks first, of course,
> > has no recourse for their claim.
> > They are obviously too eager.
> > They never get their way.

> > > For the game to persist,
> > > those who are present must admit:
> > > no hunger, no want, no claim;
> > > no regarding the lone biscuit
> > > which has little warmth left to it.

> > > > My uncles are always humble,
> > > > too deep in their final rambling,
> > > > to give the less than fresh dough
> > > > a second thought.
> > > > This is called the long game.

Some recognize this as a challenge.
The trick is to chuckle along, to survive,
to push through the punchlines until
all eyes have forgotten about the prize.

    In the meantime,
    the game on the side is merciless.
    We children don't play it modest.
    We may be family, cousins even,
    but that is no bond that cannot be broken.
    Our war for stale bread is truly in excess.

        My cousins will then begin,
        to lay their cards on the table:
        the youngest should get it,
        the oldest deserves it,
        the cook should claim it,
        the cleanup crew should split it.

            Sometimes they rush to clean,
            thinking the kitchen patrol duty
            will gain them more favor for their side.
            Whomever does the trash takes the cake.
            But guess how long that takes?

                It is truly silly,
                the multitudes of mindsets
                about who gets the last bread.
                While those at the table compete,
                I simply wait for the right moment -
                the still silence of the aftermath
                when every one returns to see,
                the butter crumbs on my seat.

Sunshine Friend

I saw today a great sword aglow
slicing forth from hurricane greys –
those looming walls of cumulus clouds
that spent all night shaming and blaming –
and stole the light from the front patio.

     I watched as it zippered,
     parting the rain like a knife,
     the grey walls of doom and gloom
     subsided with solemn sighs.
     It tapped on my window
     and I let it through
     watching my room come to life.

It set fire to my floor,
my walls and my bed.
It tickled my eyes,
which woke from their slumber,
and my hands, my cheeks,
my arms and my feet,
all turned pinkish red.

     My closet appeared golden,
     buying all shadows for a sale.
     When it tried on my clothes,
     releasing thousands of dust motes,
     I thought I saw an odd sprite,
     something bright with a tail.

It put on my best clothes,
even my shoes with the bend.
It held out its bright yellow hands
and sent a fever running in my skin.
"Pleased to greet ya," it said,
"I'm your new sunshine friend."

> I chuckled in my sheets
> as the warmth began to creep,
> up to the ceiling and onto the fan.
> I studied its face,
> but it was without trace,
> and watched as it turned and ran.

I chased it to the rear door,
which it set ablaze with arcs,
into the garden which yawned
and buzzed as oranges blossomed.
"Watch this," it exclaimed
and soon burst into sparks.

> The lawn lit asunder, no wonder,
> as the dawn of light blazed true.
> Where once the night time sky
> seemed to merge all and unite,
> now mirrored songs of lively throngs
> and trinkets of the morning hues.

Ebony Scales

I'm sorry to say
a snake went today
into the garden hedge
without a single care.
A beautiful black racer
with slick scaly skin,
two stripes on her back
and really quite rare.

At first when I saw
its slivering ebony nose,
I stood still as a stone
and kept my body hush.
We stared back and forth
like warriors trapped,
playing the fun game called:
freeze, flee, or rush.

I took a small step,
holding my breath in progress,
on my smallest of toes -
a spy in the night.
It blinked a few times
processing my steady skill,
wondering if it must yet again
freeze, slither, or fight.

I was nearly upon her,
and she slowly slithered close to me.
I would have really caught her, too,
but then slammed the porch screen.
My pa came up to my side
brandishing a spade in his fists,
forcing both the snake and I
to hide or flee.

I watched my dear friend,
a beauty with dark glassy skin,
slither and slide in the grass.
If only she could fly.
She had no fighting defense
to block the spade lance,
so the game came to an end.
My pa asked me why
I chose to stand there and cry,
while he held my friend in his hands;
dangling dead like a spaghetti strand.

Drizzle

A sliver of sepia light,
suspended on a silken strand,
casts about minute shadows
as it wavers with the slightest
of breezes from my ceiling fan.

Frayed threads of airtight thoughts
stir behind my slumbering gaze,
as if mildewed and molded, heavily
encumbered by the constraints of
meteorological constants - summer rain.

At three o' clock the sky closes up,
sending a drizzle of humid mist.
Tinkling drops careening softly
like the wetting of a filbert brush
before the first of many flicks.

Leaves on dogwood trees,
supplanted by a dripping spritz,
faintly tip their beaks with care,
pouring forth a fine limpid stream,
painting freckles upon the grit.

One Degree

I think I must skip school today,
I'm not feeling all too well.
My head is spinning,
my stomach whinnies,
and my bones hurt quite a lot.
My toes are red,
and my fingers creak,
my tush is sore
and my nose does leak.
I really think
this might be the end for me.

My hair is frizzy,
my skin tingles like mad.
My eyes are dusty,
my teeth feel grimy,
and my voice has gone all bad.
My chest feels heavy,
my lungs are smithereens.
I must stay in bed,
and rest my weary head;
I really think
this might be the end.

My temperature reads
ninety-nine degrees.
I'm as hot as a burning star!
I promise, to honest,
today's test 'aint the reason
I won't enter my mum's car.

Hillside Water Slide

Here I sit above the clouds
clinging tightly to my suit,
looking down, down, down –
far below the lowest ground –
where a flock of eyes gather round
a swirling chasm of doom.

A flume of churning waters
splashes me with an icy claw,
making me quiver in defeat.
I want to get off, off, off –
away from this death chute.
I don't see how other kids do it,
jumping and sliding,
even closing their eyes and gliding.

The line is starting to pile behind me,
no one dares go a fourth time.
They usher me forward,
pushing, prodding, poking me,
saying, "Aren't you hot?
Aren't you boiling? It's too hot
to avoid the rapid water drop."

I do admit, it is rather scorching
and with a push I am sent sliding,
down, down, down –
shooting like a water rocket –

until the slick tarp ran out
from underneath my bum.
When then I ran as fast as I could
to relish another go,
another chance to try
the hillside water slide.

The line wrapped down the slope
and I thought it would never end.
"I waited for about ten minutes,
is it time to go again?"
At last when I arrived,
and I was ready to fly on my back,
the hydrant hose ran dry and coarse
and all I could do was quack.
"Hey! Turn it back!"

Rink Romance

Rolling fast on inline skates,
like slowly sailing fifty feet.
Zipping and weaving through
couples holding hands,
children hugging walls and crawling,
and parents who impatiently stand.

Around a left hand bend,
I turn sharp and send it -
I put all my weight into my plan -
elapsing and racing the narrow straight,
to pass close by my crush with haste.

I passed them thrice already
and each time I caught their eye.
Their smile grew ever so slightly
whenever I whizzed right by.
It is a show of speed
and they must catch me,
but usually, they shake
their head and give a sigh.

The disc jockey announces
the final contest of the night:
five lucky contestants
will compete for a prize.
It is always a free entrance,
which would usually suffice,
but today I have a one-track-mind.

To race Tall Patrick, whose legs

stretch long and skinny,
I need to grow a pair of wings
and send fire from my bearings.
I must eclipse his feathered footsteps
and surpass him in three roller rinks.

When the music beat dropped,
Tall Patrick took off
with a speed as fast as a car.
I gathered behind,
attempting to drift in his dust,
putting pizza fueled energy
into my roller-blade thrusts.

Round and round,
nearly gaining ground.
Tall Patrick seems to be letting up.
The finish line is ahead.
I think I've got this, I may have won!
But Patrick taps my shoulder
and says, "You have only finished lap one."

The rink returns to free skate,
and my crush sits on the side,
I am defeated, I am not worthy,
but I attempt my final try.
My crush smiles and laughs,
poking fun at my busted dream.
I turned away dejected, deflated,
but then they gave me ice cream.

I guess losing to Tall Patrick
'aint as bad as I thought it to be.

Disgust

You know those things
with the wriggling wings
and the importance of a slug?
With a reputation of foul beasts
some believe they are the dirtiest bug.

This is partially true,
as they do swim in filth,
but I wish they got some credit
when I tell others the bit -
about how they shower less than
this bug cleans their abdomen.

I know all about their nature,
their courting and collective behavior,
how even some creepy crawlies
are really older than they seem to be.
Though I know this is more
than the average person believes.

I'm sure my family thinks I'm nuts
for being curious about this bug.
Especially when I leave them be
and my sisters tell me, "kill it please!"
before they scuttle beneath the closet rug.

I know you must also think
that I'm odd to have this approach.
But even you must respect,
the recoil in your chest,
when you hear the word, "cockroach."

Bear Hug

Don't let go,
we've only forty minutes.
Hug me tighter,
or the world might slip away.

Move to the side,
left foot, then right.
Don't let the basketball game
break our stride.

Across the hopscotch squares,
together lets try our best.
Don't let go.
This is only a test.

There goes the bell,
the gym coach has that look.
She's trying to pry us apart,
but the crowbar wont work.

The warning bell rings
five minutes until next class.
Coach is furiously trying
to break our glue-like grasp.

Let's stand here all day,
and skip the whole year.
As long as we're stuck
in this infinite hug,
I am your bear, dear.

Impossible Creatures

Another wild safari hunt
where our shoes slip
on mushy, gooey muck;
down the creek
where box turtles sleep
and push themselves across.

We brought our jars
for trapping moths
and spoons for scooping
up nasty moss;
where the tadpoles wriggle,
making us giggle,
for they have barely any toes.

My friends are spotters
and I'm just a squatter,
for I don't mind the slush.
When we hop into the mud
they point to some crawling crud,
pretending to be trainers
with pocket ball containers,
saying a turtle has a water gun.

A battle of wits begins at once,
a duel of imaginative throws.
We hoot, holler and shout out loud,
"Catch it fast! Before it evolves!"

Anthony goes to claim his prize
to begin his lifetime journey -
he wants to be a monster trainer
but we are all short of money.

Bending over to scoop through goop,
the creature sends him crashing.
For even though his skills were strong
you cannot catch a snapping turtle.

It's hard to tell what actually played
through the four minds present -
perhaps we all thought it best
to say nothing about our visions.

I only declined to speak my mind
'cause a bit of moss came crawling out.
It said to me, "I'm a fightin' flower dog.
My leaves are sharper than steel cogs."
In reality, I knew that it could not talk,
but I huddled close to its stalk,
petting a budding sapling sprout.

Camera One, Camera Two

One hot summer day,
I was gifted a beat up box.
It was as silver as mica stone
and took grainy photos of anything –
the puddles on the sidewalk,
the blades of grass in the sun,
a photo of tangled trees,
and my sibling's hand showing peace.

The silver box with a rumpled edge
took the world in splendid scenes.
I took it everywhere I thought I could,
to the playground of my youth,
the waterlogged storm drains,
the overgrown forest,
even the atlantic beach.

Then came a day
the shutter stopped clicking
and the box grinded to a halt.
I took it apart like a surgeon
cleaning grains of sand,
and flecks of dirt,
dried bits of salty ocean,
even a bit of mossy murk.

I thought I was ready
to turn the world back to song,
but, you see, I lost a screw, or two,
and the box stopped turning on.

I told my pa, who just shrugged,
"You should have asked me
to fix it first, but…"
He tossed the silver box aside
and brought out a gleaming pride -
a red machine with a fancy lens.

I hugged him once and set right off.
I did not want to miss a shot.
I clicked and clacked every detail,
the dewdrops on the garden hose,
the anthills full of flames.
I shot just about everything
that I could not give a name.

A macroscopic lens for viewing
gave me brand new thoughts.
I turned that box onto my skin
and captured a hundred pale dots,
the hairs on my arms,
even a sugar ant who crossed.

Then came a day
after two thousand frames,
where I stood in a ruddy beck.
I forgot it tends to rain
cats and mice every day,
so I went home soaked in cloud sweat.
To top it all off,
I had a frog in my socks,
and my new red box got wet.

www.ingramcontent.com/pod-product-compliance
Lightning Source LLC
Chambersburg PA
CBHW032030090426

42741CB00006B/797